THE
SCHOOL BUS

MARGO GATES

GRL Consultants,
Diane Craig and Monica Marx,
Certified Literacy Specialists

Lerner Publications ◆ Minneapolis

Educator Toolbox

Reading books is a great way for kids to express what they're interested in. Before reading this title, ask the reader these questions:

What do you think this book is about? Look at the cover for clues.

What do you already know about riding the school bus?

What do you want to find out about riding the school bus?

Let's Read Together

Encourage the reader to use the pictures to understand the text.

Point out when the reader successfully sounds out a word.

Praise the reader for recognizing sight words such as *for* and *out*.

TABLE OF CONTENTS

The School Bus. 4

The School Bus

We wait for the bus
at our bus stop.
We stand on the
sidewalk.

The bus is here!
Its red lights flash.
They tell cars to stop.

We make a line.
The bus driver
opens the door.

8

What other things do
you stand in line for?

We hold the handrail as we climb the stairs.

The bus has a lift.
The driver lowers it
for a student who
uses a wheelchair.

We sit in our seats. We keep our backpacks out of the aisle.

Why is it
important to keep
things out of the aisle?

The bus pulls up to school.
When the door opens,
we get off the bus.

STEP

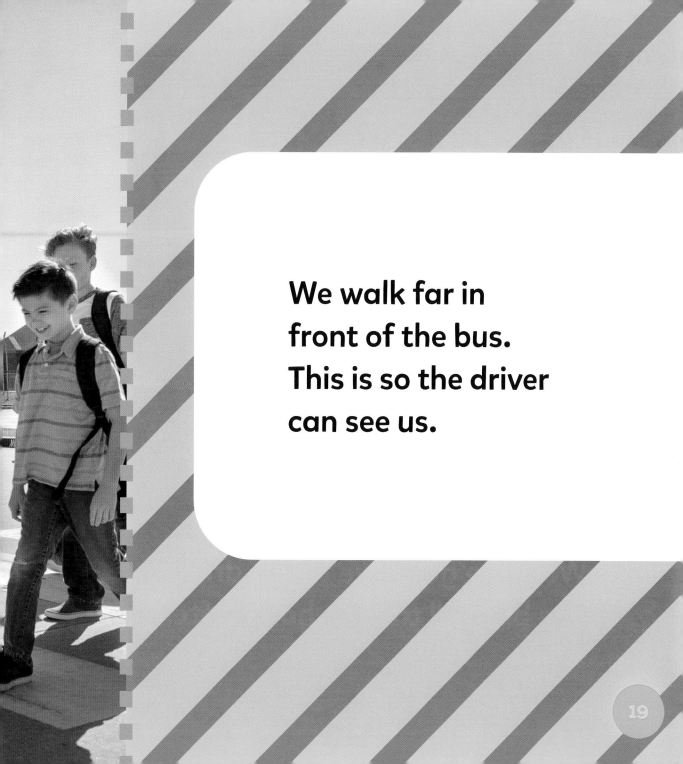

We walk far in
front of the bus.
This is so the driver
can see us.

We wave goodbye to the driver.
The bus will take us home after school!

You Connect!

How do you get to school?

What is something you see on your way to school?

How do you stay safe on your way to school?

Social and Emotional Snapshot

Student voice is crucial to building reader confidence. Ask the reader:

> What is your favorite part of this book?

> What is something you learned from this book?

> Did this book remind you of your own bus rides?

Opportunities for social and emotional learning are everywhere. How can you connect the topic of this book to the SEL competencies below?

Self-Awareness
Relationship Skills
Social Awareness

Photo Glossary

aisle

driver

handrail

lift

Learn More

Gates, Margo. *The First Day of School*. Minneapolis: Lerner Publications, 2023.

Mattern, Joanne. *We Go on a School Bus*. Egremont, MA: Red Chair Press, 2020.

Rustad, Martha E. H. *Tanya Takes the School Bus*. Minneapolis: Millbrook Press, 2018.

Index

Photo Acknowledgments

The images in this book are used with the permission of: © BCFC/Shutterstock Images, p. 16; © FatCamera/iStockphoto, pp. 10–11, 23 (handrail); © 4 PM production/Shutterstock Images, pp. 14–15, 23 (aisle); © jarenwicklund/iStockphoto, pp. 12–13, 23 (lift); © kali9/iStockphoto, pp. 8–9; © LightFieldStudios/iStockphoto, pp. 20, 23 (driver); © lutherhill/iStockphoto, pp. 6–7; © Monkey Business Images/Shutterstock Images, p. 8; © SDI Productions/iStockphoto, pp. 16–17, 18–19; © Yobro10/iStockphoto, pp. 4–5.

Cover Photo: Monkey Business Images/Shutterstock Images.

Design Elements: © Mighty Media, Inc.

Lerner Publications Company
An imprint of Lerner Publishing Group, Inc.
241 First Avenue North
Minneapolis, MN 55401 USA

For reading levels and more information, look up this title at www.lernerbooks.com.

Main body text set in Mikado a Medium.
Typeface provided by Hannes von Doehren.

Library of Congress Cataloging-in-Publication Data

Names: Gates, Margo, author.
Title: The school bus / Margo Gates.
Description: Minneapolis, MN : Lerner Publications, [2023] | Series: Read about school (Read for a Better World) | "GRL Consultants, Diane Craig and Monica Marx, Certified Literacy Specialists." | Audience: Ages 5–8 years | Audience: Grades K–1 | Summary: "There's a lot of responsibility that comes with riding a school bus. Instructive text and full-color photographs bring bus safety to life in this accessible book"— Provided by publisher.
Identifiers: LCCN 2021043408 (print) | LCCN 2021043409 (ebook) | ISBN 9781728459301 (Library Binding) | ISBN 9781728464237 (Paperback) | ISBN 9781728461847 (eBook)
Subjects: LCSH: School buses—Juvenile literature. | School children—Transportation—Safety measures—Juvenile literature.
Classification: LCC LB2864 .G38 2023 (print) | LCC LB2864 (ebook) | DDC 371.8/72—dc23/eng/20220120

LC record available at https://lccn.loc.gov/2021043408
LC ebook record available at https://lccn.loc.gov/2021043409

Manufactured in the United States of America
1 - CG - 7/15/22